THOUGHTFULLY

POETRY

Bob McCluskey

Printed in Canada

ISBN: 978-1-4866-0922-2

Word Alive Press
131 Cordite Road, Winnipeg, MB R3W 1S1
www.wordalivepress.ca

MIX
Paper from
responsible sources
FSC® C016245

Cataloguing in Publication information may be obtained from Library
and Archives Canada

SUNSHINE HILLS FOURSQUARE CHURCH
6749 120th STREET, DELTA, B.C.   V4E 2A7
Phone 604-594-0810 • Fax 604-594-6673

Dedication

The time has arrived when my persistently accumulating poetry must see the light of day and so, another book...Hopefully, time and experience have added somewhat to my poetic skills, but only you readers can be the judge of this, and so I beg your indulgence once more...My bride's family as well as my own plus many assorted friends, have been welcome grist for my poetic mill and my sincere hope is that I have caused no offence to any and with that hope, I dedicate this book to them all.

Thump-Thump, Thump-Thump

September 19, 2014

My heart beats in sure, perfect rhythm,
as it has for these eighty-eight years.
Thump-thump, thump-thump
Without ever a bump,
till a heart attack introduced fears.

I seem to have survived, so I must be alive,
for that thump-thump keeps thumping away.
I don't have to keep time, for this beauty of mine
undertakes on its own, with a rhythm sublime,
and with perfect deportment each day.

I know it won't thump-thump forever,
but I'll know when that rascal does stop.
For I won't hear a sound
as blood stops going round,
I'll be careful to not spill a drop.

I won't have time to reprimand him,
for they say that's the end of the line.
Well, he's stood me good stead,
I'll just join him in bed
for duration of time.

As Men Grow Old

October 18, 2014

As men grow old they still remain
Within themselves refined, urbane
The bones might sag
Reflexes lag
They struggle to not e'er complain
Quite civilized!

Nobly enticing female taste
With shoulders broad, constricted waist
This is of course, within their mind
Where, ever to themselves they find
Life courses with a measured grace
Idealized!

Still conscious of each lady's charms
They suavely muffle false alarms
When compliment's misunderstood
Intended to bring only good
To bolster lady's self esteem
To dream!

The mirror's truth they e'er deny
They're looking at some other guy
They're handsomer than him, for sure
From cruel reality, demure
So, even though the years do fly
Don't ever die!

Reclining Office Chair

October 17, 2014

In my gently reclining office chair,
with the window open to get some air,
my mind doth travel to someplace where,
I have never been before.

For the comfort found in my leather bound
armchaired reclining device,
induces sleep and its kinda neat,
how I drift away in a trice.

And the resident dreamers who there I see,
strangely enough are aware of me.
It seems as though I didst ever be, alive
amongst them there.

It seems so natural, it seems so right,
as I steal sleep from the following night.
That the dream unfolds, to the joint delight
of the residents there.

But, where do they come from, they seem so real,
as the theme of the dream unrolls like a reel.
Their features, their actions, their voices conceal
their ephemeral nothingness.

Do I make them up, they're so real it seems,
these mystery folk that inhabit my dreams.
And where do they go, when my mind careens
back into wakefulness.

My Garden Farewell

September 11, 2014

The walks wherein I once didst go
are empty now, of me.
My garden where the lilies grow
that I didst see.

Dost blossom in the years anon
without my condescend.
Geraniums that see me gone,
grieve not their friend.

For gardens grandly only see
the fashion of the day.
Another friend, no longer me,
doth occupy their way.

Displaying not, unfaithfulness,
their beauty flaunts for all.
They revelled in my tenderness,
before my fall.

And revel on they will, of course,
for life doth ever rise.
To bid adieu without remorse,
to this, my sad demise.

So radiate, my beauties fair,
I had thee for a while.
But new admirers now will care,
and water with a smile.

Villains Villainize

September 8, 2014

As dusk begins to blend,
familiar summer garden sights
where pathway once didst wend,
are less familiar in the night.

Dampness doth now permeate,
fog imitates the rain.
Invading shadows hesitate
to penetrate again.

Above, celestial moon doth ride
assuredly o'er cloud swept seas.
To reach the place where moons abide
to take their ease.

Doth movement in the shadow
reveal danger lurking there.
Must I demonstrate bravado
just as if I didn't care.

To venture out tonight without
a weapon for defence,
where villains might be just about
to villainize, without a doubt
doth not make any sense.

And so "Me Hearties", off to bed,
you've had your evening's fun.
Pull down the blind and never mind
the goblins, everyone.

Brevity

September 4, 2014

This wordiness
doth yet portray
thy manifest
absurdiness
another way.

Thy ample verbiage
of verse
doth not display
restraint.
Much better were
thy writings terse,
they aint.

So if one word
to make a point
wouldst thus suffice.
Longevity wouldst
Works anoint
From brevity,
How nice.

Matrimony

August 25, 2014

Each came to each
One momentous day
Unaware of love
In the gentle delight
Of your English way
Like a settling dove
Your visage filled me
With pure delight
As an opening day
From a darkened night
Dawned on my silence
A serenade
Flooded my consciousness
And made
A new beginning
For you and me
As now we voyage
The tranquil sea
Of matrimony

Information Pill

August 13, 2014

We absorb information
Through ears and through eyes
We learn more over time
Over time we get wise

But is this the best way
To accumulate fact
As the way most efficient
It's not too exact

If we could now for instance
Concentrate in a pill
A particular teaching
A class, if you will

A pill you ingest
It gets into the blood
Empties into the brain
We then learn in a flood

All life's pertinent points
You now learn very slow
When each brain cell anoints
Watch intelligence grow

This may sound far fetched
But that's been the way
For each brilliant idea
Since the start of man's day

We'll just have to wait
But I'll bet if you will
Someone is set apart
Stuffing stuff in a pill
To make us all smart

Summer's End

August 5, 2014

End of summer here at last,
torpid evenings undeterred.
No thought of summer loss, alas,
with passing of each lovely bird.

Off they fly to warmer climes,
displaying more inviting sense
than we might manifest betimes,
not following our avians hence.

As summer gathers tattered skirts,
displaying early how decay,
degrading such perfection, hurts,
as seasons ply their languid way.

Our garden, frayed now at the edge,
doth bravely, early mornings seek
to hide the browning of its sedge
with flagrant colors, sadly weak.

And so dear friends, we honor thee,
with hours of fragrant reminisce.
Who summers past, didst honor we
who part now, with a lover's kiss.

Ask Me No More

July 3, 2014

Ask me no more,
To ardent effort make
For certain not before
The hour I wake
Life's day runs long
Ones temper runneth short
As twilight settles in
Thy will abort
See to it on thine own
If seek thou must
If thou in safety trust
Beware of missile thrown
Involuntarily
Tread thou amidst my home
I tell thee verily
To treasure flesh and bone
Tread thou most warily
Just leave me all alone
To snuggle hairily
Into my tortured nest
To sleep summarily
Ah rest, sweet rest

Thoughtful Foolishness

July 30, 2014

What Shakespeare learned, did he learn in school,
or did he teach the teachers instead.
Did his Mom and Dad have a difficult time,
did he speak to his folks in confusing rhyme,
was the way that he talked of his own design,
or did it come from something he read?

When Shakespeare was seven, his mother and dad
had a terrible time with his speech.
Shakespeare, it's time you got into your bed,
"dost thou require my so early demise", he said,
"thy cruel favor exceedeth thy reach".

Shakespeare, you'd better watch over your mouth,
or I'll wash your mouth out with soap.
"Thy insidious threat to disparage free speech
with an agent to cleanse where thou canst not reach,
is a flagrant discharge of man's hope".

That's it, you're a very disobedient child,
whatever it was that you said.
Dad, the board of education, must be applied
to his seat of learning, it can't be denied,
what on earth will we do with this kid.

But Shakespeare endured, we are now well assured
past limitations imposed on his youth.
He conversed in such a peculiar way,
people only just learned what he meant, today,
now his flamboyant English is on display,
we have learned he was telling the truth.

Stirrings Deep Within

July7, 2014

Dreaming, scheming older men,
who somehow seem to strive.
For prominence, vainglorious,
whilst yet they're still alive.

These stirrings deep within,
rise up unbidden, unaware.
To steal their peace, to never cease,
tho no one seems to care.

What doth bestir the poet, Sir,
when he would rather sleep.
Who gives a damn, for also-ran,
with destiny so deep.

Poetry as such, doth almost seem,
a rhythmical affair.
Tho oft called art, will then depart,
like insubstantial air.

And so, we see the scrivener hunched,
in abject concentrate.
It mattereth not, he will not stop,
tho hours runneth late.

So men more practical we hope,
will harbor some concern.
To bring them bread or lay their head,
to rest, they'll never learn.

This Tiny Ant

July 3, 2014

This tiny ant, what motivates
To cross my patio, doth fear
Compel him (I assume he's male)
To venture oh so close, come near
My hugeness on a trackless waste
To helter skelter there with haste
Is it because he's told he can't
This ant

This tiny ant, he is so small, so wee
He seems to have no fear of me
Is he aware of me at all
Of hearing seems bereft, I call
To no avail, he wanders on
Why doth he search, what seekest he
It can't be honey, he's no bee
This ant

This tiny ant, surely must not live alone
If this were true, he'd not be prone
To reproduce abundantly
As most eloquently then do I
To his abundance, testify
There never was an ant free zone
Wherever then could be his home
This ant

This tiny ant, a sorry end didst meet
So carelessly, he walked beneath my feet
When to his end he did careen
Didst emanate an ant like scream
How lurid be imaginations
He's severed now, all ant relations
His ant friends never more will greet
This ant

Upside Down Folk

June 30, 2014

I've been puzzled by something, not something I ate,
its the speed at which this planet earth doth rotate.
Little more than one thousand miles racing, per hour,
continuing even when I take a shower.

Which puzzles me deeply, I haste to confess,
all that water at speed should be making a mess.
When I go for a walk, not a hair out of place,
Why doth not that high speed rearrange my nice face.

That centrifugal force should propel into space,
perhaps not the fatties, but most in this place.
Then, if you keep on walking and walk out of town,
you'll eventually see folk, just hangin' around.

If you walk till you get to the bottom of earth,
their feet all point upwards and have since their birth.
With their heads pointing down
'cause they're opposite us,
If we kept our position we'd cause quite a fuss.

And the water in oceans tries hard to get out,
when the moon starts to pull
and the waves give a shout.
Why the Antarctic ocean away down below,
doesn't drop to the sky, I guess I'll never know.

So I gave it all up, I'm not slated to know,
how those folk just keep hangin' around down below.
But I do thank the Lord, it's not my place to see
why centrifugal force maketh mystery.

Restoring Purity To Clay

June 2o, 2014

Ah the earth, where man's debauch,
Was then absorbed yet never watched.
Digested, cleansed, restored again,
Contributing to man's domain.

Where does the filth and poison go,
somewhere within, way down below.
God's great design prepares the way,
restoring purity to clay.

Which brings me to my present theme,
distasteful though, as it might seem.
Each body, ever born to earth,
inevitably, must life reverse.

Where the elements in man return,
back to the soil, bury or burn.
In untold billions, burdening
long suffering soil, whether peasant or king.

So potatoes eaten by someone,
were nourished perhaps, by Napoleon.
Did that rutabaga baked or fried,
spring from Shakespeare, after he died.

Now, we won't berate your imagination,
or further stifle your indignation.
But next time you sup, just think perchance,
who those vegies bring to remembrance.

Tin Ear

June 12, 2014

What think ye of the telephone
That decorates most every home
That innocently cares to sit
Upon the desk that harbors it
Up tight, alone

Awaiting opportunity
To pounce upon our backs
He knows that very soon if he
Is patient, sleeping we will be
Then he attacks

And not too softly, if you please
His hammer drives us to our knees
As we are startled wide awake
With great delight he deigns to break
Our ease

Harshly demands we take his call
As in our rush we almost fall
His urgency seems life or death
As we're responding, out of breath
About it all

You can imagine my chagrin
As voice enquires if Mable's in
I'm alone, no #%*+? Mable here
My anger blasts into his ear
His ear has turned to tin I fear
As hunt to locate Mable dear
Must again begin

Passing Train

June 12, 2014

Have you noticed,
The things you strain to see
As you're traveling
In the train with me
To focus as things flash by
You try
But they go out of focus
Wandering by
Your window pane

Things like a light
In a passing abode
Though the houses don't pass,
Its the train you rode
That passed by
That streaming yellow light
Glimpsing you rocketing
Through the night
As the landscape flowed

Must I again state
They don't flow at all
Those houses are anchored
With basement and wall
It's you that's flowing

In speeding coach
As the noisy train brings
Great reproach
At even's fall

But not to worry
You were not meant
To witness every passing event
There I go again
The events don't pass
They're anchored
In stone and wood and glass
It's you that's passing, I iterate
And if they don't hurry
You're gonna be late....Again

Who Knowed

June 7, 2014

The years have slowed
The former trivia that flowed
No longer are related to
By those of us now bowed
Who knowed

Not you, you say, don't go away
It's slowly creeping up on you
And when it comes you never knew
Forgetfulness was here to stay
Perhaps today

Oh, you won't notice much at first
Your patience thinks its gonna burst
From your vain search for something lost
Its principle, its not the cost
Damned liverwurst

But never mind, after you swear
You'll find you didn't really care
Why you must find that meat today
Relax, you only have to pray
Its waiting there

You won't remember what, before
You came into the kitchen for
Then after your perverse retreat
The light goes on, you hid the meat
In humidor

Green Thumb

May 22, 2014

Some folks have a green thumb,
a garden to preen thumb,
which seems quite delightful to me.
They just nip off the dead blooms,
the "its time to behead" blooms,
thus setting each nascent bloom free.

They have greatest capacity,
enhanced by audacity,
bringing dead deserts alive.
If on me it depended,
'twould soon be suspended,
no matter how hard I might strive.

They declare it their duty
to create great beauty,
being fated to labor unsung.
Thru the heat of the day
they just garden away,
till they're old
tho they start out quite young.

So the lesson my friend
if on you we depend
to ensure that our gardens stay green.
You must set your fee higher
to damp our desire,
we'd then value you more, not demean.

One Winter's Eve

October 28, 2014

I came to her one winter's eve
as snowflakes fell at night's o'erflowing.
Heart's intent, to ne'er deceive
on such a lovely winter's eve,
with open fireplace glowing.

But rather, to declare my love
as I approached with fervent shaking.
Heart aflutter, eyes aglow,
barely able now to know,
was courage strong enough for undertaking.

Stern father then came into room,
ensconcing in his favourite chair.
His presence underscored my doom,
if he did not leave pretty soon,
I'm out'a there.

Peering through the window, I
endured fear's palpitations.
If shaking ceased not soon, I'd fly
away from there, to not apply
a union betwixt she and I,
which subsequently would deny
our future generations.

Her father left, I window tapped,
she screamed, my courage quickly snapped.
He chased me with his forty-five,
I'm lucky to be still alive.
Another girl and I contrived
to wed not long thereafter.

Where Mind Meanders

October 27, 2014

Where doth mind of man meander
Untethered by designs, awake
What thoughts unbidden, slyly enter
Sleeps accommodating state

Thoughts relating then to naught
Which otherwise couldst maketh sense
That, ether voyaging, were caught
Ere starry winds propel them hence

To silently, in black and white
Eject from sleeping mind, awaking
Flying then through starry night
Another's sleep slyly o'ertaking

Where they now wouldst be invading
Mind of other sleeping soul
To some receptive head relating
Tales in part but never whole
As silent sleeper grants control

Swift Passage

May 15, 2014

As a babe we start mewling
From both ends we're drooling
Then reluctant to school
Acting up as a rule
While the stuff of youth seeming
Delightfully steaming
The heat of desire
Doth induce a large fire
Youth quickly doth pass
Seeming never to last
Where the price of the game
Declaimed, not worth the candle
As middle age came
With no babies to dandle
Just present a corsage
Before daily massage
Or fulfill thy duty
With basket quite fruity
And then advance again
Into age with a cane
Lying down at the end
A sweet rest to intend
But they think you departed
The last rites they started
And this you will rue
They'll throw dirt over you

Shakespeare Indeed

May 14, 2014

Shakespeare indeed!
Lived there any other name by higher fame decreed!
The weariness of time hath thus advanced
His honor to the heights of writ enhanced
And scattered this largess on which we feed

No other standard's elevation rose so high
All literature hath broadened sure
Emboldened by such regal nomenclature
Which lesser fools belatedly decry

While this unlettered fool doth boldly praise
Such brilliant, glaring genius
Although never before seen thus
Even in my grossest ignorance
This unfamiliar Shakespeare doth amaze

And so, with these closing lines I do thus plead
Shakespeare indeed!

It's Only Me Inside

April 25, 2014

Ah, the indolent, halcyon, idle days of age
When men are motivated less by greed
Lost appetites reduce the need to feed
And splendidly sartorial, greys the sage

When wisdom doth prevail, man's words be few
Pontificating doth not come to fore
Then sensing that great wisdom lies in store
Man doth await each utterance, wouldn't you

And so, man doth await each splendid quote
Each pearl that droppeth from those saintly lips
To gather all sage utters, thus equips
These lesser mortals, knowledge to promote

And so this old deceiver ever loves to stay
Well hidden, no one knows its only me inside
Where supposedly great wisdom doth abide
If they ever knew, then me and maybe you
Would be sent off to Coventry today

Where Does They Go

May 12, 2014

Reclining in my garden, spring is here, spring is here,
barren winter staggered back the way it came.
Oh, its waiting out there somewhere,
out wherever winters go,
just so its not harassing me, its all the same.

I was seated whilst perusing
the cold juice my wife was juicing,
philosophically thinking of the ants.
Who, whilst I let down my guard then
they in force invade my garden,
sore intent to make a salad of my plants.

Then, as my eye began to stray,
I noticed not too far away,
Bug varieties in numberless degree.
There were large and there were small,
some you couldn't see at all,
They were foraging with valor,
which imposed on me, a pallor,
looking closely, I'm sure I detected glee.

There were bugs with a proboscis,
they insert and suck a lot with,
bugs that bite and bugs that sting,
bugs that drag a funny thing
out behind them but they never seem to mind.
Which, when I accidently stepped on,
they just nonchalantly kept on,
didn't seem to miss the loss of their behind.

Now, the question I would ask you,
after finishing their tasks, who
can tell me where they goes to spend their time.
When the sun has gone to rest,
I would offer you this test,
do they have wee, tiny houses,
where at night they just carouses
while they plans to eat those flowers, which are mine.

The greater mystery I would vent,
when the ground becomes cement
as the winter wraps us up in freezing cold.
They're too small for heading south,
though I hear by word of mouth,
undetected, unsuspected,
they seem to always have selected
a warm place within my house, or so I'm told.

In the Still of the Night

May 11, 2014

In the still of the night,
my army mounts its wailing steeds,
to charge into the fray.
Where buildings burn,
or somewhere else the city bleeds,
while I just sleep away.

In the still of the night,
fire engines race and cruisers wail,
as ambulances poise for flight.
While thieves would desecrate my treasure trove,
my army
mounted, madly drove, to carry them to jail.

In the still of the night, my army fights a hidden war,
against men's evil hearts.
I know not what induces them,
whatever do they do it for,
thank God they play their parts.

In the still of the night, while sleeping safely in my bed,
their sirens penetrate my head, as I come half awake.
They put their lives right on the line,
so I can safely live with mine,
complaining of the noise their sirens make.

In the still of the night, policemen find a man shot
through the head,
his killer fled the scene.
A tiny hole between the eyes,
back of his head blown off as there he lies,
the sight turns hardened cops a sickly green.

In the still of the night,
ambulances wailing to a three car accident,
will clean the bloody mess.
They save the living, gather body parts dismembered
from the dead,
while police complete their agonized assess.

My army mounts up while we sleep,
as bravely, civil peace they keep,
protecting us, they fight the righteous fight.
Peace Officers are aptly named,
as evil men they keep well tamed,
in the still, still depths of the night.

Honey Just for You

April 25, 2014

Honey! Have you thought of it
While eating that big pot of it
Do you suppose the lie is true
Bee made that honey just for you
And not for it

He labors long and hard you know
Tediously, each blossoms glow
Sustains him for long hours on end
His foraging does not depend
On you, you know

He has those baby bees to feed
And locked within his genes, the need
To function in his social group
And baby bees will not eat soup
Or seed, you know

And winter bringeth snow, you know
When flowers will not grow, you know
Bees cuddle up in one big mass
Until the winter cold doth pass
It's true you know

The year begins, it's no big deal
The honey they produce, we steal
They know not who's the thief, you know
That brings them all that grief, you know
It's quite beyond belief, you know
It's you, you know

Love's Tale Retold

April 12, 2014

When hearts do pine alone for love
Doth heartbeat falter
Doth lonely heart seek God above
As substitute for human love
On lost hope's altar

Had we the gift of inner sight
Would we see hearts abandon
Years of trial to get it right
Hearts weakening from fear or fright
With little left to stand on

Is love the nourishment sublime
To keep hearts beating
Do hearts abandoned over time
From hungering for love sweet clime
Become unstable in their oft repeating

Ah! Balm of love doth now assuage
A hungry hearts sweet pain
When arms, a slender waist engage
Romantic love hath set the stage
For love's sweet story ever told again

Lost Song

April 4, 2014

A poet labors over words
Words that must express the thought
Which comes unbidden, unrelenting
From depths long hidden, circumventing
Until caught

Words describing past affairs
Broken, golden in the sun
Gut wrenching, but who really cares
When poets offer up their wares
To anyone

Wretched hours laboring
Through labyrinthine mind channels
Sweet memories gently flavoring
The come and go of thoughts
Unending flow

The hour late, an empty plate
Crass words that tend to deviate
From every channel set upon
The session ends without the song
No one will ever know

Old Men

March 8, 2014

Men, without much effort,
as they graduate through life.
Are favored with authority,
not to flaunt superiority,
that would not be nice.

Its just a mantle they're afforded
and it fits them like a glove.
They don't demand it, Its just given,
with a conscience ne'er riven
by unkindness, only love.

Then the years perform their duty,
leeching energy at will.
They could always fix each problem
till encroaching age doth rob them
of solutions to fulfill.

While the spirit might be willing,
flesh increasingly is weak.
They just sit there reminiscing,
can't remember what they're missing,
right this moment, as we speak.

As they fade into the background,
other people pass them by.
They've become inconsequential,
life is placid, uneventful,
look, they're fading, wave goodbye.

So Young

October 30, 2014

We strolled together,
She and I In ages past
So young,
We knew we'd never die
This did forever, justify
Loves sweet repast

Holding fast
To each eternal now
Each moment to devour
We knew that
We would ever be
Ensconced in radiant ecstasy
From hour to hour

Whenever then
Didst fervency decline
So carelessly
To commonplace
From dream divine
When I was hers
And she was mine
In memory

The gracious mist of time
Doth render now
Back to ancient aching hearts
Their youth somehow
Love's sweet recall
That brings back all
Those youthful years
That youthful mad eternity
We realize now
Could never be
And that's the reason
Now, that we
Shed ancient tears

My Desire Is On Fire

October 25, 2014

My desire is on fire
For the times long past
When the name that inspired
Was Everlast
When communication
Was privately kept
When we worked all day
Then untroubled, slept
When the start of a job
Became a career
And the working slob
Could afford a beer

Now the job for the slob
Is just part time
And communication
Is robbed off line
We now buy pills
to stay awake
Then pills to sleep
For heaven's sake
Our food's in a can
And many display
A bottled tan
On a rainy day

We rush to work
Then rush back home
Our pace seems governed
By metronome
We blindly stumble
Mechanically
There's hardly time
For a hurried pee
So stop the world
I want to get off
You'll be happy to see
The back o' me

Poetisizing

October 24, 2014

One day in quiet contemplation,
lap-top lit in front of me.
Sipping on some mild libation,
coffee hot, most probably.

I sought my muse for motivation,
poets in the days of yore.
Sat so, with quill and aggravation,
poetasizing evermore.

Poetic labor yesterday,
was infinitely quite intense.
Candles must be lit, no light switch,
ere poem writing might commence.

Sitting with quill poised and ready,
waiting for some thought to come.
Hand must be unshaken, steady,
ink doth blot, so cumbersome.

Then when inspiration seemeth
to, in empathy unleash.
When lost time, poet redeemeth,
memories abruptly cease.

And so, a tribute here extendeth
to compatriots of old.
As through modernity I wendeth,
computerizing, I am told.

Junk-Food Diet

February 16, 2014

I notice that lately my memory's fraught
With things to remember that I forgot
There was something to do and I almost caught
The vaguest of hints but then I would block
Everything out of my frustrated mind
Though I search and I search, I'm unable to find
The wispiest vestige of anything sane
That would give me a hint, not even my name
Then my daughter arrived and proceeded to make
A change to my diet, bananas and cake
Small pizzas presented on cardboardy trays
With endless bags of potato fillets
All crispy and crunchy and colorful too
They reminded somehow of the sole of a shoe
But hallelujah, my memories back
I'm no longer enduring a memory attack
I just place my finger on the side of my head
Close my eyes and remember all that I read
Like the co-efficient of a quaderangled square
Is equal I think to the seat of my chair
So thanks to my daughter, my memory's returned
I'm now eating the diet I formerly spurned
When I go to the store I'll remember to get
All this new junk-food....If I don't forget

To Juggle with Words

February 25, 2014

To juggle with words is a skill
One must struggle to master until
With a rapier like thrust
Or epee if you must
One can sever man's savor at will

To develop this skill, consummate
One must learn not to spurn but relate
For the reader to be-
come enamored of thee
Thou must lure him with love, never hate

For with honey is victory gained
No fly ever, of sweetness complained
You'll catch many more flies
But I'll never surmise
Why the catching of flies is ordained

So with rhyming declining to this
To proceed as if nothing's amiss
It has left me to be
Like a squirrel up a tree
Consorting with nuts in my bliss

Mr. Ecstasy

February 13, 2014

A quiet fold lies in the lee
of verdant aspen, where with thee
we oft wouldst dally pleasantly,
whilst hid beneath our favourite tree,
we three.

Mr. Ecstasy wouldst join our tryst,
though uninvited, never missed.
Wouldst ever know the day, the hour
to rendezvous, to join in our
conspiracy.

We wouldst not ever hope to know
His coming, ere his verdant flow
wouldst interrupt our sole intent,
to simply talk awhile, wouldst vent
his power on me.

And then, ere I could even think,
he'd work his magic, in a wink
we're lying in each other's arms,
examining each other's charms
with ardent glee.

I now must close this poignant tale,
no prying eyes may pierce the veil
surrounding our delightful hour
ensconced within this torpid bower.
Except of course, our favourite friend,
delightful Mr. Ecstasy.

Away We Go

February 1, 2014

Hidey Ho, and away we go
It's you and me
To forever see
The love there be
In the afterglow
Of a perfect union
Designed by God
Where we two together
Must needs applaud
All the love we know.

We fit together
Like a jigsaw puzzle
As we sit together
And just kiss and nuzzle
With nose and lips
Like the Eskimo
We're joined at the hips
And I'll have you know
If one of us slips
Down both of us go

But it works out fine
Because most of the time
We just recline
In chairs side by side
That tilt and slide
By grand design
Made extra wide
To fit at the hip
For you and me
As we watch T.V.
Then to bed we go,
Goodnight, sleep tight
Happy Hidey Ho

Dream Life

February 1, 2014

There is something we see of loveliness
so oft in a passing glance.
From no one we know, in the endless flow
of passersby in life's frenzied dance,
just chance.

For the briefest moment, eyes touch and go
onward in life, where we could not know
ever anon, for the moment's gone
to delectable heavenly afterglow,
a lost hello.

As far as we are able to see,
nothing was ever meant to be.
To follow up as a consequence,
to linger upon doth make no sense,
reflectively.

These passing moments in life doth seem
less like reality, more a dream.
And in truth, tho frequent they're oft forgot,
relegated to a remember-me-not,
that doth not matter, to never demean.

And yet, what inscrutably different lives
in retrospect, might have ever occurred.
But in living were never meant to be
in our wildest imaginations, lest we
appear absurd.

Self Doubt

January 29, 2014

Good writers they say, always suffer self doubt,
from that empty white page when a novel starts out.
Whatever the genre, seems always the same,
they begin knowing little, except maybe the name,
even that in the end, might take rout.

So what about poets, to which I make claim,
though as poet elicited, what's in a name.
Be that as it may, let's get back to the point,
I suffer never self doubt, as myself I anoint
with sobriquet, poet, and intend to remain.

For the thing that I suffer, is never self doubt,
since each poem I start is completed without
trailing off into nothingness, simply absurd,
to rhyme, in good time there is always a word,
tho inane, in the brain of this sensitive lout.

And so it would seem, by that yardstick they tell,
self doubt should identify good poets as well.
Be off with thee varlets, I'll not condescend
to accept condemnation that doth grievous, offend,
I resist with my back to the wall, to the end.

Words

January 17, 2014

Words, like golden drops
hold precious meaning.
Syllables with open tops
though, spill themselves
when over leaning.

Words expressing
vague contempt
for formalism, appliquéd.
Will offer up a contretemps,
as hidden recognition vents
against a contradiction made.

But in the end,
vague words, my friend
sometimes when they
are over leaning,
lose the meaning
they intend,
as cross the page
they move, careening.
In the end
they just offend
the ones they hoped
to be redeeming.

Nothing Doth Match

January 25, 2014

Growing old brings with it, different truths,
unexpectedly they intrude.
Most things that would formerly stimulate,
don't even arrive 'cause I'm sleeping late,
while the world is coming unglued.

And then, around about maybe noon,
I arise and have a good scratch.
I put on the clothes I wore yesterday,
no one notices I'm dressing the same old way,
and care not, that one sock don't match.

Things that I should have done yesterday,
I notice still hangin around.
There's always something that has to be done,
which is fine as long as I'm not the one,
I stay quiet, make nary a sound.

But there is one thing I can do without,
you won't want it either, when you get old.
It's something that precipitates the gout,
makes me swear, when I forget I'm devout,
and that's ravaging, savaging cold.

So, I gotta have heat, revivalist heat,
recovering, smothering, mothering heat.
It's the only thing that settles my woes,
if you keep it coming, my life's composed,
and I'll live to a hundred, at least.

My Box

January 24, 2014

Retrospect, it would seem to me
At the end of life is a luxury
that allows one to indulge oneself
In "what might have been".
But, when I descend from life's splintered shelf,
I'm alone at sea.

Alone, of course is an acronym
for Ably Living On No-one Else.
Which we know of course simply cannot be,
for the world we enter when initially we
cause our mother's pelvis to spread so she
can eject us onto that splintered shelf,
commands that we live dependently.

So obviously, all must agree.
we do need mother, we've no one else,
but upon our descent from that splintered shelf
we're thrown out on the open sea.
That sea of course is the sea of life,
thrown out on our own, no kids or wife
we start out with an empty box.

As life goes on we throw into that box
Things desperately needed, like booze and rocks
of sweet cocaine to disguise the pain
we feel from our life at sea.
The first thing in the box, disguised on the floor
was the love that our mother placed there before
but we never knew it could be.

Now, as life ebbs down all the things I would need
are discarded one by one.
All the things in the box I now find were just greed,
And I take them out with the utmost speed,
till the box seems empty once more.
But a lovely lady, came late to my life,
I don't know why, but she's now my wife,
And I shower upon her, the love I found
hiding deep in my box, on the floor.

Ravages of Time

January 19, 2014

However may one ever,
with sad observing eye,
look upon life's seasons
without finding there, trite reasons
to, with certitude deny
the march of time.

For, the evidence, tho charming,
can for some, be most alarming
as life's inescapable ravages reveal.
Some among us all, however
unmistakably do weather
time's most ruthless, sad endeavor
to degrade with sag and line.

Some emerge at end of journey
with a countenance serene.
With an inner, radiant beauty,
from their lifelong call to duty,
of righteousness and holiness
that is not often seen.

But I wed a prime example
of a woman who shows ample
evidence that demonstrates
exactly what I mean.
My lovely octogenarian,
although at times, contrarian,
my lovely Agnes Mary,
she's my current reigning Queen.

My Plaintive Swan Song

January 16, 2014

What is this surging, desiring inside
that seeks to escape, to insatiably relate
to conjectured admirers, who fail to evoke
a concrete response, a la meaningless smoke
which doth never subscribe.

Each new beginning, each poetic gem
which is grandly presented to others
but then, fades into latent obscurity when
some immediate, pressing requirement smothers
their chance to enjoy the pursuits of my pen.

Just as the poet expressed sad care,
that his poetic roses were blooming unseen.
My flowery blooms, not ever would deem
to waft fragrance on anyone's desert air,
if you know what I mean.

So alas and alack, I must struggle alone
in my airlessly, carelessly, circumscribed home.
Like all beggarly poets, I scramble to find
enough paper and ink to unburden my mind
of it's unceasing drone.

And if you should happen to stumble upon
any scraps of my work that the wind blows along
by way of your path in your daily pursuits,
please be gentle, please rescue, partake of the fruits
of my plaintive swan song.

Winter Garden

January 16, 2014

I ventured forth in my winter field
where a casual eye would see,
a death that could not possibly yield
a flower again for me.

For winter death lay cold and spent,
would the promise never come.
Of color and scent where memory went
when earth was romanced by sun.

But my spirit man in the end began
to envisage garden delights.
And though snow didst fall to conceal it all,
extravagant visions of blossoms tall,
filled my dreams of summer nights.

As I stood entranced in my reverie,
I'm sure it was bees I heard.
Drawn by the scent, that sweet element
that lures the bees, to the blossoms intent,
though I know this appears absurd.

But for what it's worth, that vision's birth
was very real to me.
When my sense returned, the scene still burned
deep in my ecstasy.
But I knew I must go when the falling snow,
reminded, it's almost twenty below
as the house was beckoning me.

Boyhood Love

January 14, 2014

Boyhood love, how charmingly inept,
the struggle to effectively express
his boiling heartfelt secret, too long kept
contained within his ardent loneliness.

Consumed in every part with burning fire
he, bursting with audacity to be
the object of her gentle heart's desire,
would gladly die, would that but make her free.

Or any noble sacrifice, he'd gladly make,
wouldst tolerate all pain to succor her.
All self promotion, gladly would forsake
to shield her from all harm that might occur.

But then as time wears on and ardor wanes,
they drift apart as loves are wont to do.
Years later, married fatherhood ordains,
faint memory of early lover's names
are lost to Romeos like me and you.

Cart Before the Horse

January 13, 2014

What seek thee, with thy wanderings,
dissatisfaction's silent goad
leadeth to beyonder things,
to tempt by seeming fonder things,
further down life's road.

Thy gaze extendeth far away,
beyond that which closely flows.
Presenting now with forthrightness
to eyes afflict with sightlessness
for that beneath thy nose.

Fields far away, furthest afield,
appear to be the greenest yet.
Though fields surrounding
soon be abounding
more sweetly green when wet.

Wet with tears of sad remorse,
shed for that which might have been.
Thy wagon placed before thy horse,
prevaileth not in life, of course,
but backwards doth careen.

My Love For You

January 10, 2014

My love for you grows endlessly,
tis nurtured by your love.
Your loss would be the end of me
if you went on above.

Our nurture flows unbroken
through the silence of our way.
But it's surely just a token
of my love for you this day.

My love for you will never die
it surely will live on,
in all the poems I write to you,
for comfort when I'm gone.

Young Vibrant Mind

December 27, 2013

So what do you see, an old woman?
Grey hair that's increasingly thin?
You can't see the young mind
so completely confined,
to old age's undeniable chagrin.

But the eyes so perceptively able
to see youth behind living's disguise.
Are the eyes that began in the heart of a man,
that are gifted by love without guile or élan
and will not ever countenance lies.

For truth is life's ultimate arbiter,
many treasures lie hidden behind,
a sweet elderly face
where a smile can't erase
evidence of a young vibrant mind.

Compensation

January 9, 2014

Time brings compensation
it would seem, as people age.
No longer favor inclination
to seek after new sensation,
as we totter t'ward the grave.

We carefully review each step,
research what life's about.
We rest a while,
then with a smile,
decide we'll not go out.

Tomorrow is another day,
let's not rush into this.
Although we should go to the store,
we're Ok 'till tomorrow, for
the freezer holds some fish.

And so the days meander by,
all blending into one.
Decision makings mystify,
our attitudes within belie
life's seeming lack of fun.

But fun is how you make it
and we have our secret ways.
It depends on how you take it,
Every doubt hath truth to slake it,
or so the good book says.

Lost Dreams

January 7, 2014

Cold is the wind that blows,
over shattered hopes undone,
by reality of life imposed
when maturity's begun.

Warm was the wind of hope
that launched a thousand dreams.
But the darkness leaves the failed to grope
in futility, it seems.

But some there are, who will nurture, warm
those first bright rays of hope.
Who will chase the dream, who always seem
to overcome, to cope.

But where go the optimistic youth
who allow the dreams to fade.
Who settle for less, who then confess,
they stopped to watch the parade.

But I guess there has to be someone
who will work in the dirt and grime.
Who'll step into the breach to be the one
to answer the call on time.

These are the guys who drive the trucks,
who work with hammer and spade.
Who help the wife, who prevent strife
by ensuring the bills are paid.

So, here's to the dreamers, we need them too,
but we need the workers more.
Dreamers forge ahead, create the new,
but someone has to run the store.

Hospital Stay

January 1, 2014

A young girl in our ward
Was obstreperous
Justifiably denied
She was leprous
She was really just fine
We found out in time
Just sweet and benign
Like the rest of us.

So What, Then, Is Art

December 26, 2013

So, what then is art?
Well, you tell me.
Cannot art be a part
of all that we see.

All that I intentionally
present as event
for the world to see,
created by me.

If I say it's art,
does that not make it so?
Does that not then impart
a legitimate flow?

In the very same vein,
what is poetry?
Though the writer abstain
from temptation to see
himself artfully,
how can he know?

If he starts with a poem,
but ends up with prose.
If he calls it a poem
why should any propose
any other conduit
than he himself knows,
as my history shows.

So whether it's painting
that looks quite absurd.
Or assembly of verbiage
that should never be heard

What it looks like or sounds like
to his jaded gaze or my tinny tin ear,
doth the artist amaze and the poet endear.
So, I must don more fluently anger, I fear,
this poem surely is art, do I make myself clear.

I Feel I Know the Poet, Poe

December 19, 2013

The poet Poe, unkempt, unshaven,
wrote a poem about a Raven.
When he started out, I know
he had not the slightest notion
in the midst of mind's commotion,
what unseemly locomotion
would compel his mind to go,
off in unforeseen direction
with very little introspection, he knew not,
nor would I, I know.
And so I sit in daylight bright,
(Poe was writing in the night).
My window opens on a copse,
of colorful forget-me-nots
artfully so interspersed,
amongst the woods and in my verse.
Revealing then to all and sundry,
reading as we sit rotundly,
the truth about my writing skill,
that rhyming I would like to kill, or worse.
So be it, let's get on with this, this yawning,
poet's cold abyss,
which writers, Poe as well was cursed,
except of course, the ones deluded
by deep and colorful research,

which renders this poor wretch, excluded.
But turning now with great aplomb,
(I keep a bag full here at home),
to task at hand which seems to be,
imposed by I myself on me.
My effort now is to display to everyone this very day,
my friend the mouse.
My friend hides out amidst the trees,
he pokes his nose out by degrees
because he knows that lurking there,
a hungry fox maintains his lair
not too far from my house.
But even though this danger lies right there
before his little eyes,
with brave aplomb he ventures to,
come visit as he, this fear defies.
(I scattered for him some aplomb,
remember, I've a bag at home.)
He creeps up to the house and will,
agilely reach my window sill,
to perch up there as he surveys,
my wantonly debauching ways, until
overcome by curiosity,
and tempted by the crumbs I spill, he stays.
Now, mice be nervous, we all know,
and would not ever bravely go
so carelessly to hie
before a monster human's window or his door.
But tempted by the crumbs I gave, and feeling

inordinately brave, he gave in,
and trembling (tho not from the chill),
he waited on the window sill, until
I quietly invited him. Then tentatively,
much afraid a tyrant's trap was being laid
he entered in. He tip-toed to my desk with the,
hair trigger set if he must flee,
accepting then a cup of tea, he kept his beady eyes on
me, and likely inward prayed.
But bye and bye he saw that I no motive held, ulterior.
Relaxing now,
he knew somehow that I did not regard a mouse as
somehow, too inferior.
So we then had our tete a tete, discussing items,
this and that. With questions like,
have you a cat, or, will tea incite a belly ache,
I watched as little mousey ate.
But then the time came, as it must,
our fearfully accomplished trust, to abdicate.
Our mousey climbed then down the wall,
what I saw next though did appal.
I saw the fox with crafty grin, manoeuvring to pounce
on him, as mister mouse
with furtive look crept through the woods
and o'er the brook, I saw the fox
with slavering jaw devour the mouse and lastly saw
my friendly mouse's frantic look,
as fox washed him down with drink from brook,
his last hurrah!

Boxing Day

December 26, 2013

There's an unexplainable imbalance,
in the volume of traffic's degree.
It is after all
a decidedly small
afternoon foray
that I'm driving today
on a Thursday at three.

Why is the traffic so heavy,
do these people have nothing to do?
To relieve my dismay
at the traffic's delay,
I now know why they're driving
the animal way,
cause it's Boxing Day at the zoo.

My Dog Spot

December 17, 2013

I had a dog
His name was Spot
He used to chase
The cars a lot
One day, to duck
He just forgot
He was my dog
But now he's not
I miss you Spot

The Girl I Prefer

December 17, 2013

The girl who will fulfill my life sir,
is the one who will never bring strife, sir.
The girl who won't gloat at another's mink coat,
these nefarious ends she would never promote,
she's the one I would take for my wife, sir.

Now, the girl who sees me as the answer,
to her need for a steed, a high prancer.
Though she pamper and paint,
her high prancer I aint,
you fulfill her desire for romance, sir.

No, the girl who's attractive to me, sir
is the one on the hunt but low key, sir.
She doth slowly instill
her insatiable will,
as she tenders her cups of slow tea, sir.

I desire that her fire's indiscernible,
to pretend she don't care, unconcernable.
When my guard I relax,
is when she then attacks,
dragging me to the church, unreturnable.

Soporific

December 14, 2013

As I lay on the beach
Soporific
The heat from the sun
Feels terrific
But the trouble, merci
At least, it is for me
The skin that I'm in
Will quickly begin
To burn off
To be very specific
The solution they tell me
Must be
As I perambulate
By the sea
Apply lotion by hand
Do not lay in the sand
Else the pain that you gain
Aint terrific
But the end's
Really not worth the candle
Which end you might ask
Did I mean
It's the end that don't burn
As I gingerly turn
And race home
Without any preamble

Expurgated Version

December 14, 2013

You bought a book the other day
Should have thrown the thing away
The unexpurgated version
It most certainly was not
Should have taken an excursion
To a lake with an inversion
The expurgated version
Would have had a better plot
If you desire to be salacious
With a girl you deem curvaceous
You will not succeed by reading
You will never be succeeding
For you my heart is bleeding
False unexpurgation hurts a lot
If you're looking for some action
And you can't get any traction
You will get no satisfaction
Without broadening your scope
There is only one solution
You must ask for absolution
Then find girls in distribution
And marry one, you dope

Mighty Computer

December 14, 2013

The pen was mightier
Than the sword
We were all
Of one accord
Down through
The generations
Manufacturing
Creations
That contained
Their own reward

But now we have
Another suitor
An unfailingly
Straight shooter
I herald thee
My new computer
My precise
Unconvoluter
Mightier by far
Than written word

So accurately
Contending
To communicate
For you
To delete
Or to repeat
Or to instantly
Renew
Never manually
Erase again
Who knew

Tax Collector

December 13, 2013

The tax collector's
a terrible curse,
he even taxes
my empty purse.
His disposition
I'd love to axe,
but when I swing,
his head retracts.
He lives again
another day,
my diminishing money
to tax away.
But I'll get him yet
when he isn't looking
over his shoulder,
momentarily forsooking
his customarily
careful defense
without customary
common sense
when his dinner's cooking.
Then he'll be sorry,
Oh yes he will.

He'll dance like
a headless chicken until
he crosses his heart
and says he's sorry,
brings back my cash
in a great big lorry.

Do I Know You

November 26, 2013

I know a person,
Or I think that I do
But when I look in her eyes
I can't see right through
Who is she really
Down deep inside
Why are her secrets
So easy to hide
But I've found out a secret
I'm happy to share
Though you won't really know
Till you have an affair
An affair of your own
In the moralest sense
Love demanding commitment
To vacate that fence
And it means that your heart
Must be opened real wide
You must stand there naked
With nothing to hide
Show her all of your warts
All your flaws on parade
If she shows you all hers
Then pal, you've got it made
....For life

Conscious of Others

November 21, 2013

Because I am conscious of others,
Are they then any more alive?
Or conversely, if my consciousness
of them's unaware,
does their selfness less ably contrive.

You say of course, they are very alive,
their existence depends not on you.
But what if, of them no one was conscious
in the whole world, would it still be true,
would aloneness itself misconstrue?

To take this a little bit further,
since they're very, yes very alone.
If alone, with nobody to whom relate,
they would surely miss someone to love or hate,
of what consequence then, if he was a she
or if for that matter, this she was a he.

So, if everyone might on me depend,
just a little, to know they're alive.
I'd best be conscious of them, just relate,
let them know that we'd love to integrate
with each other, existencewise.

Le Pomme De Terre

November 16, 2013

Away we go, away
To the market, lackaday
We're off my dear
We can't stay here
The pantry's lacking
We must be packing
The vegetables look queer
In appearance, very sere
And I do surmise
From all of the eyes
On le pomme de terre
As they're lying there
That they're staring back at me
For they would much rather be
Mashed or fried in nice hot fat
But it's rather much too late for that
They will suffer from regret
When we throw them out, my pet
All of the effort they made to grow
Is wasted from now on I know
I can't stand to look in their eyes
A potato looks so sad when it dies
Please execute them fast
I don't want their pain to last
Let's hurry out of here
To buy new candidates my dear

A Falling Tree

November 15, 2013

Within a forest rank and bold
I watched a tree grown very old
To fade so imperceptibly
I wondered why I felt so cold
Watching ancient trees unfold
Observing God's assembly

Decay enveloped unawares
As bark fell off the tree
Though leaves were yellowing and few
I had a great concern for you
And never hardly even knew
That falling tree was me

Winter Rain

November 14, 2013

Pregnant and sodden, November unloads,
her husbanded deluge on reclining earth
into open mouths of sewer bled roads
and parched farmers fields,
exhausted from bounty of summer's yields,
and the rank extravagance of nature's birth.

Rain's curtain as seen from mountain tops,
brings a shimmer to midnight city lights,
distorting silhouettes of cars and shops
and raising the earth to meet the sky.
Or rather perhaps, to lower the sky,
down to the earth where winter nights
bring promise of shimmering Christmas lights.

While down at the shore of our ocean bay
where city tumbles to water's edge,
we stand in the rain with utter disdain
for the silence and emptiness of the day
transformed into midnight's wet display
of freighters roosting like giant cranes.
Through the drizzle they hang suspended there,
in the silent night as we start to care
for the penetrating winter wet,
and hurry now through the rain to get
home to our fire to dry out there.

Hidden Secrets
October 15, 2013

The object of dreams
And of visions divine
Unresponsive it seems
At least most of the time
The source of nutrition
Indispensible too
For man's early condition
For nourishing you
Relegated as well
To be objects of lust
I'm reluctant to tell
But I will if I must
Satisfying your search
For the secret's source
The lovely, seductive
Sweet visions of course
Are the secret delight
Of every man's quest
To obtain if he might
The sweet female breast

Promises, Promises

September 27, 2013

Just yesterday, it had my name,
a promise with the mailman came.
Anticipating great reward,
my nervousness you could not blame,
content was most engaging.

A promise they did there record,
I hungrily read every word,
They promised they could now retard
my unrepentant aging.

This promise so attracted me,
it couldn't be a faker.
As any fool could plainly see,
'twas like a miracle maker.

So, thought that I might take a chance,
but something made me look askance.
The envelope's return address,
the local undertaker.

Persecution Complex

September 9, 2013

There's a mystery I'm burning to mention,
all my life all my joints were well oiled.
I could swing, I could run like a son-of-a-gun,
life was good, I'd been terribly spoiled.

Now my joints all scream out for attention,
every movement eliciteth pain.
For my arm to reach back, brings a painful attack,
I'm reminded, don't do that again.

Now, my complex is not persecutive,
it's suggested in fact, that I'm stoic.
I just blushingly state, it's a strong irritate,
while pretending to be quite heroic.

To the point of this missive I'm coming,
if impatience you'd kindly forbear.
When I had no pain, no attention I'd gain,
as I functioned with nary a care.

But now everyone's so attentive
that I have no desire to get well.
Folks all think I'm so brave from impression I gave,
If you don't betray, give my secret away,
then I certainly never will tell.

Time To Philosophize

September 19, 2013

Ah, the strident inner rage of a man,
as the hungry years steal life away.
His inside spirit defies his fears,
as strength succumbs to fleshly decay.

The plans for life, he made without
the need to consider at length.
He could do it all regardless of doubt,
before time diminished his strength.

His step was sure, his hand was strong,
each task at the end of the day,
was ever completed with consummate skill
before time took passion away.

But although he just sits around a lot,
with a body that's closer to dead.
You'd hardly know he's alive although,
he is hard at work in his head.

For he never had time to philosophize,
while racing from task to task.
But now that he's wise, he would love to advise,
all you'd have to do is ask.

But no one much cares to abide with him,
to empty his bountiful cup.
He'd be glad to share if you'll tarry there,
just shake him to wake him up.

Poetry Gift

August 22, 2013

There rises up in my soul betimes
some thought expressing itself in rhymes,
it may be only a couple of lines
but it grabs me right where I live.

And I must be quick else the thought will fade
and I'll quickly forget the impression made
by a stern impulse or a light charade
and the pleasure it briefly gives.

Then away I'll go with a Hidey Ho,
as line by line doth quickly grow.
Tho how it will end, I never know,
it spontaneously lives.

When it finally achieves its appointed end
through twists and turns I could never intend,
recounting a tale as the words all blend,
I rejoice in the pleasure it gives.

What is this gift from a poet's heart
that just percolates up unbid at the start,
but never fails to at last impart
a spice to the life he lives.

As I Expire

October 30, 2014

To thee I pledge my troth
I do it purposely although
Despite impending fickleness
Thy temporary tenderness
Doth bless, I trow

Enough for me
The idle times you grant
In hidden bowers
Where ecstasy extant
Fills temporary hours

One day
My reach may
far exceed my grasp
and in that fateful hour
I thankfully do ask

Thy memory stay
With me a day
To while
The emptiness away
As I expire

War Of Mice And Men

August 10, 2013

Upon a night I sat engrossed
In front of my computer post,
as was my wont, for sleep evadeth me.
When from the corner of my eye,
something furry flasheth by,
so fast that I had hardly time to see.

A little mouse with bold intent,
on some important mission sent,
abruptly stopped and looked at me in awe.
He didn't seem to suffer fear
but also made it very clear,
he didn't feel at ease with what he saw.

I stared at him but didn't move,
I knew that he would not approve,
he stared at me as quietly we sat.
I thought then I heard a squeak,
I know that's how a mouse would speak,
was he enquiring if we had a cat.

My listening then became intense,
for I was curious as to whence,
my understanding of his speech did emanate.
Then when I spoke a word to him,
he seemed to know my every whim,
conversation we could now negotiate.

Quietly so as not to scare,
I asked if he would like a chair,
to equally see eye to eye with me.
He scurried up a table leg to table top so we'd engage,
in conversation much more comfortably.

I asked him for his given name
and he said thank you all the same,
but Mickey must not be his appellation.
Use Michael to engage he said,
I'm regarded as a sage he said,
by each mouse within my rodent population.

By now we're getting down to facts
and I can tell by how he acts,
that he's started to feel right at home with me.
Would he fancy then a bite,
of something tasty here tonight,
some Roquefort, mayhap with a cup of tea.

Roquefort sir, would be a blast,
I can't remember sir, when last
I was able to partake such delicacy.
So kind of you to offer me,
cheese and crackers with my tea,
I prefer tea in a saucer, if you please.

After nibbling our repast, we then settled down at last,
to enjoy a conversation, deep in thought.
Would you tell me Michael dear,
is your domicile quite near,
Or is a space behind my wall the most you've got.

Sitting on his little bum,
upon my table where he'd come,
cleaning whiskers with his tiny little hand.
He twitched his pointy nose,
and said to me I don't suppose,
that you have capacity to understand.

Throughout the day we're out of sight,
but then when you're asleep at night,
my friends and I enjoy our lovely house.
And we do assure you that,
we are so glad you have no cat,
to interrupt our nightly grand carouse.

But there really is a wall
between mice and men, so tall,
we cannot converse again, I must entreat.
You and I did break that law
and some compatibility saw,
But nevermore must you and I e'er meet.

And so it pains me now to say,
that I must quickly be away,
I have enjoyed our little tete a tete.
We cannot meet like this again,
and this causes me some pain,
for the war of mice and men I really hate.

And so adieu my friend,
as our detente comes to an end,
be assured, our parting brings me great remorse.
But we both will still maintain,
this villa as our joint domain,
Though you know we must not meet again, of course.

Look for other volumes from
poet Bob McCluskey's prolific pen:

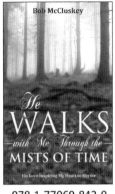

978-1-77069-842-0

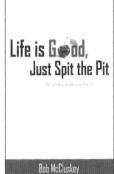

978-1-77069-735-5

978-1-4866-0930-7

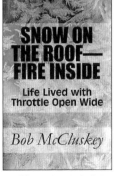

978-1-60749-840-7

978-1-77069-873-4

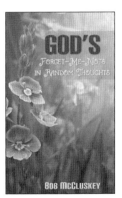

978-1-4866-0926-0